handing on the faith

Other ***Handing on the Faith*** titles:

Grandchildren

Child's Name

Birth Date   Baptismal Date

Child's Name

Birth Date   Baptismal Date

Child's Name

Birth Date   Baptismal Date

Child's Name

Birth Date   Baptismal Date

Child's Name

Birth Date   Baptismal Date

Child's Name

Birth Date   Baptismal Date

When You Are a Grandparent

Carol Luebering

ST. ANTHONY MESSENGER PRESS

Cincinnati, Ohio

Scripture citations are taken from The *New Revised Standard Version Bible*, copyright ©1989 by the Division of Christian Education of the National Council of the Churches of Christ in the United States of America, and used by permission. All rights reserved.

Excerpts adapted from the English translation of the *Catechism of the Catholic Church* for the United States of America copyright ©1994, United States Catholic Conference, Inc. Libreria Editrice Vaticana. English tranlation of the *Catechism of the Catholic Church: Modifications from the Editio Typica* copyright ©1997, United States Catholic Conference, Inc. Libreria Editrice Vaticana. Used with permission.

Cover and interior illustrations by Julie Lonneman
Cover and book design by Mary Alfieri

Library of Congress Cataloging-in-Publication Data

Luebering, Carol.
  When you are a grandparent / Carol Luebering.
      p. cm. — (Handing on the faith)
   ISBN 0-86716-488-3 (pbk.)
   1. Grandparents—Religious life. 2. Grandparenting—Religious
aspects—Catholic Church. I. Title. II. Series.
   BV4528.5 .L84 2002
   248.8'45—dc21

                                        2002002026

ISBN 0-86716-488-3

Published by St. Anthony Messenger Press
www.AmericanCatholic.org
Printed in the U.S.A.

Contents

Introduction

When I met my first grandchild, I scolded my older sister for not telling me how much fun becoming a grandparent would be. "I did tell you," she replied. "But you didn't tell me it would be *this much* fun," I retorted. "I *did* tell you," she insisted. "You just weren't listening."

Grandchildren, as well you know, are indeed one of life's sweetest gifts. We wanted nothing but the best for our children, but we fumbled our way through guiding them to adulthood. We worried about many things: health, discipline, education, the scars we might unwittingly inflict. To our lasting wonder, our children turned out to be capable, likable adults in spite of all our uncertainties.

And now they have crowned our efforts with a remarkable reward: grandchildren. We certainly worry about these kids, but we do not bear the heavy responsibility of making parental decisions for them. We are free to love these precious people without distraction just as they are. We are makers of ritual for them, guardians of family traditions and the people who can tell them stories from the past.

The following pages explore how naturally nurturing our grandchildren's faith fits our role as grandparents— and how much joy we can find in doing it.

Grandchildren are the crown of the aged....
(Proverbs 17:6a)

Knowing
the Limits

I boast that my job description as a grandma is just one word long: Enjoy!

There are, of course, a few drawbacks. One is often imposed by distance. My oldest grandkids live many miles away; I see them only a few times a year. Now we keep in touch by phone and E-mail, but when they were little, I had to start our relationship from scratch every time we met.

The more serious drawback is the dark side of the very lack of responsibility that makes being a grandparent such fun. We do not have to decide big issues like medical care or schooling for our grandkids. (Most of us don't, that is. If you are a custodial grandparent, this book is not for you. You are handing on the faith as a parent.) But neither can we make decisions about something of vital importance to us: their religious formation.

Some of our offspring grew up with deep and secure faith. We rejoice that they choose to worship with us, and we celebrate the milestones in their children's religious life. But all too often we know a very different reality.

Many young people, using the freedom God gave all of us, have abandoned the faith our generation tried so hard to hand on to them. We may find ourselves tiptoeing across a field of eggshells whenever the subject of religion arises.

You may have grandchildren who are receiving no religious education at all—even grandchildren who have not been baptized. We grandparents cannot single-handedly fill that lack. However tempting it may be to baptize a tot in the kitchen sink, it is no solution. In the first place, church law limits that right to cases where someone is in imminent danger of death. (A friend of mine did baptize a mortally ill grandson. When she admitted her action after the child's death, his parents surprised her with their thanks.)

If the child is in danger of death, it is to be baptized without delay...even when the parents are opposed.... In other cases, the parents, or at least one of them..., must consent.... *(Rite of Baptism for Children*, #8)

More importantly, baptism is not a magic act. It is an expression of faith—a parent's faith, in the case of a very young child—and, like a tiny seedling, it must be tenderly nurtured if it is to come to maturity.

Ultimately, of course, faith is God's gift, not the doing of either parent or grandparent. And faith, even though it is defined and lived in the community we call church, always has a personal dimension. Our faith may differ from our parents' in many ways. Neither is the faith any of our children holds a copy of our own.

▶ I have heard many faith stories.... And the more stories I hear, the more convinced I become that they are unique and personal. God does not call us on the same journey.... There are many paths to God. (Thomas Richstatter, O.F.M., *The Sacraments: How Catholics Pray*, St. Anthony Messenger Press, 1995)

▶ Grandparenting is new territory. We have some learning to do. We are not in charge of the parents or the parenting. Our relationship with them has changed. Pitfalls will be avoided by giving thought to the effect of our actions or responses.

Along the way we grandparents learn the value of exercising an incredible amount of tact. We regularly bite our tongues and zip our lips. (Dr. Lillian Carson, *The Essential Grandparent: A Guide to Making a Difference*, Health Communications, 1996)

▶ Those who gratefully acknowledge the faith as their greatest possession, the deepest truth they know, cannot but wish to pass it on. *(A New Catechism: Catholic Faith for Adults)*

Yet because our faith is *ours,* we have the right to articulate the beliefs we hold with or without support from our children. Wise grandparents articulate their differences with parents to the grandchildren in much the same way they say, "I like asparagus; your mother likes carrots," even though the difference is vast.

We nurture our grandchildren's faith not by trying to replace parents or prove them wrong, but by doing exactly the sort of things grandparents do best: happily being ourselves with the youngsters.

The Journey to Faith

Most of us, and our children as well, were baptized as infants and slowly brought to full participation in the church over a period of many years. But that is not the only route. The church insists that the *Rite of Christian Initiation of Adults* (RCIA, for short) is *normative:* the pattern for coming into the church.

The RCIA process is a long journey, and the path a child follows to adult faith corresponds very closely. The RCIA is separated into several stages. The first is a period of inquiry or precatechumenate—a time of searching and questioning, of tentative exploration of the Catholic faith. Preschoolers, with their eager curiosity about everything parents think and do, are very like the adults in this stage of the RCIA.

The second stage, the catechumenate, lasts a year or longer. The inquirers are formally enrolled as catechumens, signed with the cross and presented to the assembled believers at Sunday Mass. During this time they explore the Scriptures together, learn Catholic teaching and get acquainted with the community.

School-aged children go through much the same process as they gradually learn about Jesus, the people who preceded him and the believers who follow him. For youngsters, the process takes many years, and the sacraments of Eucharist and confirmation are milestones they pass along the way.

The final stage, which begins after the catechumens have been initiated, goes by an awkward Greek name: *mystagogia.* The word refers to the "mysteries" of the faith on which the new Catholics reflect intensely. They recall their experience at the Easter Vigil, consider what it means to them to share the Eucharist and seek ways to live out their commitment as disciples of Jesus. For the newly initiated, this period ends with Pentecost. In a real sense it is where all baptized believers spend the rest of their lives.

Providing Support for the Journey

Adults in the RCIA process have many companions for the journey: the catechists who explore the Sunday Scriptures and the church's belief with them, their fellow searchers, a sponsor chosen for them from the parish community and a personal sponsor who will stand as godparent, usually a person who sparked their interest in the church.

Whatever religious education our grandchildren are getting, they need many guides for their journey toward personal faith. And we grandparents are ideal for the task! The God who gave us free will, the option to reject religion, also sprinkled the world with invitations. Any of them can bring a person to adult faith: awe at the beauty of creation and at the human role as co-creators, a sense of gratitude for life's joys, a thirst for comfort when sorrow darkens the world, a hunger for meaning. But the single most important factor is surely the influence of believing people whose lives overflow with love. And our grandchildren know us as loving.

▶ By virtue of his soul and his spiritual powers of intellect and will, man is endowed with freedom, "an outstanding manifestation of the divine image."[8] *(Catechism of the Catholic Church, #1705)*
[8] *Gaudium et spes* 17.

▶ ...[S]tarting from...the world's order and beauty, one can come to a knowledge of God as the origin and end of the universe.... *(Catechism of the Catholic Church, #32)*

Furthermore, we hold a special place in our grandchildren's hearts, just as they do in ours. They are eager to learn what makes us tick. They are hungry for the living history we possess. The memories we are weaving with them and for them today they will carry all through their lives. They will draw on the traditions they absorbed from us when they have children and grandchildren of their own. We are for them a crucial link in the faith-tradition that goes back two thousand years.

Faith, as the saying has it, is more caught than taught.

The best we can do with our grandchildren is the same thing we did for our children: expose them and trust God to do the rest.

And God does work in mysterious ways. My first two grandchildren were baptized before their parents dropped out of the church. I grieved when they passed the age for first communion, but I kept my teeth set firmly in my tongue (a good grandparenting skill!) and waited.

It was the children themselves who sought a solution. Long before she reached puberty, my granddaughter began attending church with a friend; she and her brother were both always glad to go with us when we were together. She was instrumental in reawakening her parents' interest.

One day their parents started both kids in CCD; they soon made their first communions. The little girl's interest in music drew her into the children's choir, much to her father's pride.

A friend who coordinates the RCIA in her parish tells about a family of four who came to ask her about entering the process. When she probed their reasons, this was the story they told:

The oldest child, a young teenager, had also been attending Mass with his peers. He was so entranced with what he found there that he brought his little sister with him. Their dad had grown up in the church but long since abandoned the practice of his religion. Mom had never professed any faith. They began going to church with the kids and came to the RCIA to learn more.

"A little child shall lead them," Scripture says (see Isaiah 11:6). Who but God knows where our grandchildren may take even our errant offspring?

For Reflection and Discussion

* *Recall your own journey to adult faith. What persons and events had the greatest influence?*

* *How was your relationship with your grandparents different from your relationship with your parents? What was special about it?*

* *What do you enjoy most about being a grandparent?*

Children as living members of the family contribute in their own way to the sanctification of their parents. *(Pastoral Constitution on the Church in the Modern World, #48)*

The world is charged with the
    grandeur of God.
It will flame out, like shining
    from shook foil....

(Gerard Manley Hopkins, "God's Grandeur")

Mirroring God's Love

The Scriptures cherished by Christians and Jews describe God in parental terms. God is the *Abba* of Jesus, Isaiah's mother who can never forget the child called Israel (see Isaiah 14:15). Yet the picture of God one little girl drew in her first-grade religion class bore no resemblance to her parents. She drew an old man with white hair.

"You know, I think God looks a lot like me," her grandpa teased her. "Of course he does," the little girl replied. "God is *really* old, and he has pockets full of surprises and he loves me even when I'm bad."

Chalk one up for the small theologian! However hard we tried, as parents we seldom displayed the same bemused patience that God lavishes on the fractious children of the human race. We loved our kids no matter what, of course. But in the day-to-day business of caring for them and feeling heavily responsible for how they turned out, we didn't often simply rejoice in who they were.

Grandparents, on the other hand, are more tolerant. As I told my newest grandchild, "I think you're wonderful! That's my job because I'm the grandma." As I went on to tell her that I would still think she was wonderful when everyone else agreed she was horrid, her mom began to laugh. But I wasn't joking. That was the ninth time I had made that speech to a newborn and I take it seriously. It reflects my memories of my own grandma, who always made me feel loved and special.

Reflecting God's Love

Knowing that someone loves us unconditionally is the closest we come in this world to seeing God's face. Anyone who rests secure in such a love, even a tiny infant, has already made a giant step toward belief in God. For God doesn't just love us, Scripture says. God *is* love (see 1 John 4:8).

▶ Beloved, let us love one another, because love is from God; everyone who loves is born of God and knows God. Whoever does not love does not know God, for God is love. (1 John 4:7-8)

▶ Then the women said to Naomi [King David's great-grandmother], "Blessed be the LORD, who has not left you this day without next-of-kin.... He [the infant Obed] shall be to you a restorer of life and a nourisher of your old age; for your daughter-in-law, who loves you, who is more to you than seven sons, has borne him." (Ruth 4:14-15)

Well-loved children also have a head start on learning to live a Christian life. Remember how Jesus answered the man who asked what he must do to gain heaven. Jesus summed up his people's whole belief in one commandment: Love God and neighbor (see Luke 10:25-27). Human infants grow into a people capable of loving generously only by discovering what it is like to be on the receiving end of such love.

Living God's Love

The love Jesus spoke of isn't, of course, just a matter of warm hugs and sweet words. It takes an investment of time and attention to put love into action, and sometimes it is costly. For Jesus himself, remember, love led to Calvary.

Loving our grandchildren is not likely to demand our life's blood. But it does require great chunks of time and more patience than we ever had with our own offspring.

The work begins early, when you begin to get acquainted with a tiny new person. If, like my oldest, your grandchildren are miles away from you, becoming someone real to a little one is a daunting task. Remembering that God "dwells in inapproachable light" (see 2 Timothy 6:16) and is still as close as our hearts inspires us to seek creative ways to bridge the distance.

Our first grandchild teethed on a picture of us that her mom mounted in a special frame; she listened to stories I taped for her. Maybe that helped. But mostly we had to start from square one every time we saw her in the early years. (I once heard her tell her mom, "Grandma is a stranger.")

As time goes by, of course, you can keep in touch by phone and mail, dropping cards and notes into the mailbox or making contact through cyberspace. (Even kindergartners are computer-literate these days. Our five-year-old forwarded her birthday wishlist from a catalog company.)

Whatever the distance, it isn't just keeping in touch that shows a child how God loves, but living out the promise I made my little ones: Always think they are wonderful.

An Unfailing Ally

Someone once quipped that children and grandparents are natural allies because they have a common enemy. Whether or not that is true, a grandparent can certainly be a child's best ally.

My Gram wisely held that there are two kinds of spoiling: the good kind and the bad kind. Every child *needs* the good kind, she insisted. A friend whose mother-in-law lived just four doors away tells how her children used to run down the street to Grandma's every time they were punished. That grandma practiced bad spoiling: She gave them cookies and told them how wrong Mom was.

Gram wasn't four doors away when I was a child; she moved into our house when I was nine. When I got into trouble (a not uncommon event), I always fled to her room. I knew she wouldn't come to my defense or criticize my mother; she never did. She wouldn't even offer me an orange gumdrop slice from her candy dish on such occasions.

She just let me sit there with her, listening to her stories or practicing the use of a crochet hook. All the while I soaked up the reassurance that, however wicked I might be, I was still lovable. That is spoiling *par excellence,* and it gives a remarkable insight into the way God loves the badly spoiled human race.

Extending Acceptance

The need for a loyal and loving ally doesn't diminish with the years. Teens need a lot of support in their struggle toward independent adulthood. We once grounded our sixteen-year-old son for some mischief that landed him in juvenile court. It was a stressful period: We had emptied our dining room to make room for his dying grandmother's hospital bed. Mom was a gentle soul who almost never offered a word of criticism. But as I tucked her in one night, she said softly, "You know, you can't keep him grounded forever." And I knew she was right. She freed me from my worries about her long enough to deal more equitably with our boy.

Teens tend to question many things that have always been taken for granted, from parental wisdom to appropriate styles in dress and hairdos, from moral issues to the very existence of God. We grandparents have weathered many a season of such questions, our own and our children's. We can be to our grandchildren what we are to other young folks we know: mentors who give the support gained from hard experience.

Those of us who remember the Second Vatican Council also remember lists against which we examined our conscience. They defined entertaining doubts about God or the church as gravely sinful. As life brought questions about either into focus, we learned that wrestling with such questions often leads to deeper faith. We can offer a maturing child that most precious of gifts: We can listen with patience and without judgment. (The key word here is *listen.* As one wise grandpa noted, "God gave us two ears and only one mouth to remind us that listening is more important than talking.")

Like the issues that we struggled with, teenage questioning most often has one of two centers: the suffering of innocent people and the dark side of the church's history.

The first is as old as faith. A poet of ancient Israel wrote a lengthy poem about a man named Job. Like the biblical Job, teens often wonder how a supposedly good God can tolerate wars and natural disasters, grave illness and poverty. From our own experience we can honestly say, "I wondered about that myself when..." and share the insights our struggles gave us.

The church seems a tougher nut to crack. Certainly there are distressing episodes in its history and heated divisions today.

So it has always been! According to the Gospels, Peter, the first pope, was a bungler whom Jesus called Satan (see Matthew 16:23 or Mark 8:30); when the going got rough on Good Friday Peter denied his Lord three times. The generous sharing of property that marked the new community was shattered early on when Ananais and Sapphira lied and withheld a sum of money for their own use (see Acts 5:1-6).

The quarrels began early on. When Gentiles first joined the infant church not long after Pentecost, the leaders disagreed about whether or not they must observe the Jewish Law (see Acts 15). And that was but the first heated theological debate of the many we have endured!

"The Church...will receive its perfection only in the glory of heaven,"... at the time of Christ's glorious return. Until that day, "the Church progresses on her pilgrimage...." *(Catechism of the Catholic Church, #769)*

If, as the Second Vatican Council insisted, the church is a pilgrim people struggling together toward God, its faults are easier to forgive. Our grandchildren, their parents and we ourselves are all numbered among that people. Few of us have many illusions about our perfection; we are all too aware that we make mistakes—sometimes beauts! Yet the church we love is not necessarily the flawed institution. Rather, we have found a home among the other imperfect people with whom we worship.

Our grandchildren are baptized into this community of believers. Like us, they can take heart from the folks in the pews who share their frustrations with the church as well as their love for it, who give us comfort in our sorrows and rejoice with us when life is sweet, who inspire us with their efforts to live lives of service and love.

Being open about the way we wrestled with the problems faith presents us with puts us squarely on the youngster's side. Whatever conclusions he or she may eventually come to, we will have established one certainty:

Grandma or Grandpa is willing to hear whatever a young person needs to say.

Nurturing Wonder

Wonder is the underpinning of belief. Standing beneath towering giant redwoods or caught off guard by a vivid sunset, we catch our breath in awe. We lift a newborn into our arms and sense that we have felt the touch of Someone greater than ourselves. Like Moses shedding his shoes in front of a flame-wreathed bush, we ask, "Who are you?"

Our grandchildren arrive filled with wonder, as we did ourselves. Even a tiny baby is fascinated by faces and voices and movement. Taking a walk with a toddler is an adventure in rediscovering the world: the patterns on a leaf, the quick scurry of an ant, the texture of a pebble. As toddlers grow older, however, they grow accustomed to the marvels around them, just as we did.

Yet many of the things we do with our grandchildren are invitations to wonder. We take delight in watching their eyes widen, and so we take them to the zoo, the natural history museum, the woods, the planetarium. These outings hone their appreciation of God's wonderful creation.

We admire the work of human hands with them, as well. Art museums are full of beauty, of course, but so are buildings and bridges if we pay attention to detail. Favorite books and songs sprang from human creativity, as did all the modern conveniences we take for granted. (Surely you remember your first encounter with that tool today's kids use so naturally, the personal computer.)

Small children need little encouragement to take

delight in what they can do. As we grow older, however, we develop some odd notions about humility. We begin to equate taking pleasure in our God-given gifts as sinful pride, not as reasons for praising the Giver, as true humility requires.

From the crayon scrawl you proudly hang on your refrigerator to a grandchild's doctoral thesis, praise a young person's skills and accomplishments generously. Celebrate your youngster's ability to add something useful or beautiful to the world—to be co-creators with God. Your delight helps inoculate your grandchildren against false humility.

Our newest grandchild was born on a Sunday. The Responsorial Psalm that morning addressed the God who "formed my inmost parts; …knit me together in my mother's womb./I praise you, for I am fearfully and wonderfully made" (Psalm 139:13). I thought it a perfect song for a birthday. That grandchild cannot yet understand the words. But she knows their meaning: She spends much time admiring her recently discovered hands. As she learns to use them with ever-increasing skill, I will encourage her to keep taking delight in how wonderfully made she is!

Planning Surprises

We live in Cincinnati, whose airport is just across the Ohio River in Kentucky. One delightful day we took two young grandchildren for a surprise outing. As the four-year-old tells it, we went all the way down a *long* hill through the woods to the "ocean," put grandpa's car on a boat (the ferry) and crossed the "ocean." Then we went all the way through the woods up another *long* hill and watched the airplanes take off and land. Our expedition ended, of course, at the ice cream store.

The kids had a great time. So did we! As the little theologian said, God has pockets full of surprises just like Grandpa. And, like grandparents, God enjoys lavishing them on us. Perhaps the most delightful surprise to emerge from God's pockets is the wonder each grandchild is. And perhaps the greatest surprise we can offer over all the years is our willingness to continue taking delight in these precious people.

Teaching Theology

Don't hesitate to make explicit the connection between your love and God's. Lavish praise on your treasures and thank God for the gifts they have and the gifts they are. Assure them that the time you "waste" with them gives you as well as them enormous pleasure and borrow a phrase from Cardinal Joseph Bernardin, who once described prayer as wasting time with God.

Stress the magnitude of God's love, God's willingness to accept our questions and find delight in us as we are, God's hope that we in turn will find delight in the divine Grandparent.

Above all, place your trust in the grace God lavishes on the children of your children.

For Reflection and Discussion

- *Whose love has touched you so deeply that you felt God's love?*

- *How did your grandparents make you feel special? How do you pass on this gift to your grandchildren?*

- *When can you remember getting needed support from your grandparents?*

- *When have your grandkids needed support from you?*

- *What doubts and questions have plagued you? Who helped you wrestle with them?*

[The] family is the foundation of society. In it various generations come together and help one another to grow wise.... *(The Church in the Modern World, #52)*

[The feast of Joachim and Ann] reminds grandparents of their responsibility to establish a tone for generations to come. They must make the traditions live and offer them as a promise to little children. *(Saint of the Day,* St. Anthony Messenger Press, 2001)

► I have loved you with an
    everlasting love;
  therefore I have continued
    my faithfulness to you.
        (Jeremiah 31:3)

► ...God did not make death,
  and he does not delight in the death of the living.
  For he created all things so that they might exist....
  (Wisdom 1:13-14a)

Celebrating Rituals

As she cleaned my teeth, the young woman described the meal she would enjoy on Thanksgiving Day. Her face glowed with anticipation. "We *always* have…" she began, and recited the list that is all too familiar to me. She was a living lesson in the power of ritual.

Those of us who grew up in the United States have eaten many a Thanksgiving meal, often at our grandparents' table. Before we had two digits in our age, we could tell the story of the feast the Pilgrims shared with their Native American friends and how we continue the custom of giving thanks over a similar feast. And we, too, could recite the list of foods that would be served.

The elements of the meal are constant because Thanksgiving dinner is an important *ritual* in our culture. Ritual by definition has a comfortably familiar shape. We learn the words and gestures and elements so well we never have to give them conscious thought.

We knew the language of ritual—song and gesture and prescribed words—long before we grasped the meaning of Thanksgiving Day. Warm milk from breast or bottle not only eased the pain of an empty tummy, it also had a human meal's power to forge bonds of love and trust.

The first conscious learning an infant acquires is how to make a gesture that is the same in any language: the lopsided responsive smile that so delights us. Babies learn many more rituals before their first birthday: peek-a-boo, waving bye-bye, the bedtime routine.

And woe to the adult who fails to follow the rubrics! Small children love rituals for the sense of security they provide. And they tolerate little deviance from "the way we always do it."

If you babysit a tot and can't find the best-loved stuffed animal, screams will arise from the crib. Our two-year-old wants the peel on her banana pulled back, but don't you dare to remove it. Our little grandson has to observe rituals of his own design before he will settle in for an afternoon snooze: two stories, an M&M and the door pulled to but not closed tight.

The Language of Faith

Every belief has systems of ritual. Christians fold their hands in prayer and repeat the words Jesus taught his disciples; Muslims bow to the ground and praise Allah's greatness. Jewish men don hats for prayer and their wives light the Sabbath candles. Catholic women of my generation remember pinning a Kleenex on their heads before entering a church, following Saint Paul's injunction against bareheaded females (see 1 Corinthians 11:45).

Catholic worship is sacramental. Our prayer uses the language of ritual: gestures and signs and familiar words. We use ordinary things—bread and wine, oil and water—

to express our deepest beliefs. We sign ourselves with a cross. We affirm our participation with an *amen* and express our unity in Christ with the Sign of Peace. The Sunday liturgy is as familiar to us as the bedtime ritual is to our grandchildren.

You want those precious youngsters to be just as at home with our worship. Hone their ritual skills first by respecting their cherished notions about the way things are "always" done. Encourage little ones to create rituals you can share with them.

When I put my daughter's little ones down for their nap, my grandson is quick to remind me if I omit the one thing I have added to the routine. "Grandma," he says, "you forgot about the bedbugs!" The response, of course, is "Good night. Sleep tight. Don't let the bedbugs bite." It matters not at all that neither of us has ever seen a bedbug—much less been bitten by one.

Introducing Religious Rituals

One grandma I know always traces a cross on her grandchildren's foreheads when she sees them off for home or bed. She wishes God's blessing on them and sometimes reminds them that she performed the same gesture when they were baptized. Another passes the privilege of saying grace at family gatherings from one child to another. One grandpa never gives a child a hug without saying, "God bless you."

Explore the possibilities of mealtime blessings at your table. Fold hands or hold hands. Pray the familiar "Bless us, O Lord," invite spontaneous prayer or sing a simple song. Include a prayer for those whose tables are bare or whose food is made bitter by loneliness or sorrow.

Join your grandchildren in bedtime prayers and seek other prayer opportunities. Place a container of holy water near your front door and bless the kids as they come and go. Light candles against the darkness of the headlines or as an ongoing prayer for some need—and, of course, let little ones make a ceremony out of blowing them out.

We are body-person. There is no other way for us to experience the invisible except through that which we can touch, taste, smell, see, hear, and feel. That's why ritual is so important to us. Ritual enables us to enact bodily the belief that God touches our lives in special ways. Ritual enables us to enact the faith that is within. (Sandra DeGidio, *Sacraments Alive: Their History, Celebration and Significance,* Twenty-third Publications, 1991)

Holidays invite more complicated rituals. One couple scatters crèche scenes throughout the house on Christmas Eve, but all the mangers are empty. When the clan gathers, they parade from room to room. The older grandchildren proudly lead with lighted candles, and the little ones put the baby Jesus in place.

Celebrate the Twelve Days of Christmas with your grandchildren. (Your parish bulletin or diocesan newspaper may offer suggestions appropriate to your area.) Leave your Christmas decorations up until Epiphany. End the season with a Twelfth Night party and a room-by-room blessing of your home or theirs. (Check your local religious bookstore for a pamphlet outlining a simple rite.)

Easter eggs are more than just fun to decorate. As harbingers of new life, eggs clearly have resurrection significance that you can articulate.

Look for the religious meaning of other holidays and enflesh them in rituals. Grace over Thanksgiving dinner offers an opportunity for each person to name a reason to be thankful. Devise your own ways to praise God's love on Valentine's Day, trust the dead to divine care on Memorial Day or express the value of useful work on Labor Day.

Enriching Children's Experience of Liturgy

For all my dental assistant's enthusiasm about the Thanksgiving menu, that meal is, to me, no fun to cook. The size of the crowd doesn't daunt me; it's the sameness of the menu I detest. You see, I love to cook. Every week I plan seven menus, carefully balancing flavors and textures and colors, vitamins, carbohydrates and proteins. I am happiest trying new recipes.

Once a year I prepare a huge spread that's heavy on starches and closed to innovation. It is no fun at all. (My sister, who takes no joy in cooking, disagrees. She enjoys Thanksgiving kitchen duty *because* she can go with the tried and true.)

Our worship can also bore our grandchildren. Little

ones squirm; older kids complain that they "get nothing out of it."

For very little ones, buy books (or, better yet, coloring books) about God and Jesus to take to church. Some parishes regularly offer a children's Liturgy of the Word, taking slightly older youngsters out to explore biblical stories at their own level. Shop around for one and invite the kids to join you.

If your parish or theirs has a children's liturgy on Christmas, attend it with your grandkids. In any case, take a moment to visit the crèche scene. Watch it for the Magi's arrival.

Hone older kids' enthusiasm by exposing them to the variety of Catholic worship. Start with the nearest parish that has a really good guitar group and branch out from there. My sister and her husband took their grandkids to an inner-city parish with a largely African American population. The rhythms of the gospel music and the enthusiastic preaching delighted them.

Seek out parishes in your area that celebrate with other ethnic accents: mariachi music in Latin American neighborhoods, Eastern rite congregations. Most dioceses offer a Latin Mass somewhere; call the chancery and ask. It's unlikely to engage most kids' interest, but they will be fascinated to discover how you and your parents once worshiped in a strange language.

The Easter Vigil is the high point of the church year. The service is long and cannot begin until sundown, so it isn't for very young children, but older kids may find it awesome—literally.

It begins in darkness suddenly shattered by the Easter fire. The paschal candle, symbol of the risen Lord, is lit from the fire and carried into the church, where worshippers light their individual candles from its flame.

The story of salvation is told through Scripture passages read in the candlelit church. Alleluias resound at the Gospel story of the Resurrection. The catechumens, newcomers to the faith who have been through the lengthy RCIA process, are then baptized in newly blessed water and confirmed with fragrant oil. And all of us, old believers and newborn Christians, join together in the celebration of Eucharist. It is quite an experience to share with your grandchildren.

Celebrating Religious Milestones

You will of course, be there to celebrate your grandchildren's first communion and confirmation, if you possibly can. What about first penance? You have, after all, helped them discover God's boundless mercy with your own loving forgiveness.

You will undoubtedly send gifts for those events, as well. Exercise creativity when you shop for presents. They don't have to be explicitly religious to be appropriate.

Instead of the traditional first communion prayer book (white for girls, black for boys), consider a gift like the one a friend chose. She gave the child a tambourine accompanied by a biblical injunction: "Make a joyful noise unto the Lord" (see Psalm 6:1). Other simple music-makers—drums, whistles, bells, a recorder—would serve as well. (Grandparents buy noisy things; parents rarely do!)

A carefully chosen children's Bible or book of Bible stories is a good gift. So are *Can You Find Jesus?* and *Can*

You Find Bible Heroes? (St. Anthony Messenger Press)—
and they're a lot more fun.

For first penance, a book or video is a good choice.
Shel Silverstein's *The Giving Tree* or *The Velveteen Rab-
bit* by Marjery Williams Bianco speak of the way God
loves us.

Whatever the age a child is at confirmation, he or she
becomes a fully initiated Christian with all the privileges
and responsibilities that entails. Involve the young be-
liever in the church's efforts to relieve human suffering.
Consider making a contribution to the needy in his or her
name or inviting a teenager to join you in your favorite
volunteer effort.

Introduce your young confirmand to the church beyond parish boundaries. Take a tour of your diocesan
cathedral and explore the history of the diocese. Invite an
older youngster to attend the Chrism Mass during Holy
Week and see the blessing of the confirmation oil.

The best gift for sacramental milestones (or, for that
matter, any occasion!) is the gift of yourself. Express
your delight that the child you love has made a giant step
in faith. Continue to say how much you treasure sharing
the sacraments with him or her long after the big day.

For Reflection and Discussion

- *What rituals of their own invention do you share with
  your grandkids?*

- *What family rituals have you introduced them to?*

- *What are your grandchildren's favorite holiday
  rituals?*

- *What are your memories of religious milestones in your life or your children's? How do you think they compare with your grandchildren's?*

- *What different experiences of worship have you shared with your grandchildren?*

The joy and hope, the grief and anguish of the men of our time, especially of those who are poor or afflicted in any way, are the joy and hope, the grief and anguish of the followers of Christ as well. Nothing that is genuinely human fails to find an echo in their hearts. *(Pastoral Constitution on the Church, #1)*

▶ One of the basic distinctive marks of our way of praying is *ritual:* we do things over and over in set ways, and after a while, we know what is going to happen next. (Thomas Richstatter, O.F.M., *The Sacraments: How Catholics Pray)*

▶ Catholics worship not just with their heads but with the things of earth: bread and wine, water and oil, coming together and going apart, standing still and processing forward, lighting candles and smelling flowers, even dust and ashes! That's *liturgical* prayer—prayer with the body, the earth, ritual, song, celebration. (Thomas Richstatter, O.F.M., *The Sacraments: How Catholics Pray)*

Passing on the Tradition

Throughout human history, one group in every tribe or community has been the custodians of tradition. The elders passed down the people's story to the younger members.

We don't call ourselves elders. Many of us don't even qualify for senior citizens' discounts yet. Nevertheless, our memories reach back farther than the eldest of our children can recall. We grew up in a world beyond our grandchildren's imagining. And we heard the stories *our* grandparents told. (Sometimes we didn't listen as well as we now wish we had. Many a family genealogist rues an inattentive ear.) The role of storyteller, historian and guardian of tradition falls to us.

Telling the Family Story

Children don't come with a sense of history. It develops slowly, beginning with a self-centered focus. A young baby remembers familiar faces; a toddler talks about his or her last birthday. Gradually, tots realize that other people have memories that predate their very existence. Discovering connections to the people who were family before they were born is an important step for our grandchildren, part of developing a sense of their own identity.

A year or so ago, the grandson who is now newly four struggled with the concept that we were his Mommy's parents. How hard to believe that she had ever been our little girl! He liked seeing old pictures of her and hearing stories about her childhood. Soon he was telling his mother that they were going to "your mother's house"; he still speaks to me of her as "your girl." And one day he was delighted to discover that some of the pictures on the family room wall are *our* parents and grandparents. There is a religious element to this history. Our family album holds, as yours does, pictures of baptisms and first communions and weddings—even glimpses of the churches where these events took place. My young descendants see themselves in the long christening dress that my grandmother made for my mother.

Older children want more detail. They ask when and how couples met; they are interested in knowing where their ancestors came from and what brought them to another land.

The search for religious freedom brought many of our ancestors to new shores. My dad's family were Germans enticed to settle in the Volga Valley by the Russian Empress Catherine the Great. She promised them religious freedom; when her successors reneged on the pact a century later, they set sail for America and raised the wheat that had flourished in Russia on the plains of Western Kansas.

Others didn't find the tolerance they sought. Irish immigrants found employment only as domestics or laborers on the railroad. My own Irish grandfather courted a young woman descended from English Congregationalists for eight years before her father consented to their marriage.

Some folks, of course, didn't choose to immigrate at all. They came in the holds of slave ships and still face roadblocks.

When you tell your grandchildren how your forebears reached this country, be sure to include how the parishes they built helped them both to keep precious aspects of their native culture and to find a place in the American mainstream. If possible, take them to visit some of the churches where your forebears worshipped.

I hold in my mind's eye the church my German grandfather's people built on the plains of Western Kansas. They erected a wooden cross as a worship center and then built sod homes. Once they were housed, they began a stone church. The horse that pulled the stone to the site, so I heard, knew the routine so well that he turned around and headed back to the quarry without prompting. And their little church is so beautiful that it once appeared in the pages of *National Geographic,* captioned "the cathedral of the plains."

Telling Your Own Story

I can't remember when I first heard Ruth Eleanor's name. She was my other grandparents' first child, a beautiful golden-haired baby who lived only six weeks. My grandmother was overwhelmed by grief. Grandpa's pastor, Father Gerard, tried to assure her that she had an angel in heaven who would always watch over her. Her parents, concerned for her sanity, took her to stay at their distant home. Their stern minister scolded her for not accepting God's will. As soon as she returned home, she went to see Father Gerard about becoming a Catholic.

Your own religious journey may not have been so dramatic. Nevertheless, you can surely recall turning points along the way, moments of insight and inspiration. Share them with your grandchildren.

Introducing the Larger Family

When the elders of the tribe from which Jesus sprang told stories to their grandchildren, they didn't just talk about the people they remembered personally. They spoke of Abraham and Sarah, that elderly couple who traveled far from home at God's promise of a child and became the parents of a nation. They recounted a sad tale of slavery in Egypt, of roasted lamb and unleavened bread eaten in haste, of a long and arduous journey across the desert to the Promised Land and of a mountain that trembled under the weight of God's presence. They talked about David, the shepherd boy who became Israel's greatest king, and of the promise that another, greater ruler would be among his descendants.

Christians retold the same history, reading the life and death of Jesus back into it. They added tales of the apostles and, over the centuries, of the many saintly people who answered Jesus' call to follow him.

Teaching the whole sweep of salvation history doesn't fall within our job description as grandparents. But we can put flesh on these ancestors whose bones turned to dust long before any family member whose story we know.

*[S]aints...*means not just those who have been canonized by the Church, but *all God's holy people....* Thus Paul writes to the "saints" of Ephesus and Corinth and Achaia, Philippi, Colossus. Today he would write to the "holy ones" of Chicago or Brownsville or Ottawa.... (Leonard Foley, O.F.M., *Believing in Jesus,* St. Anthony Messenger Press, 2000)

Saint Anthony of Padua was a close friend of my grandmother's. She made him a member of our family. There was no need she could not turn into something for Anthony to find. She asked him to find mislaid objects, of course. She also sought his help in finding a job for someone, a baby for a childless couple.

On the Sunday morning my dad died, my mother, my sister and I went to church after leaving the hospital. Needless to say, we wept through Mass. As we got up to leave, a woman in the pew behind us pressed a few leaflets into my mother's hand. "I don't know what's troubling you," she said, "but maybe these will help."

When we were outside the church door, Mother looked at them. They were all prayers to Anthony. Coincidence? Maybe, but we were sure we recognized the touch of Gram's comforting hand.

Introduce your grandchildren to the saints. Talk about your favorites and why those people hold such a special place in your life. Tell them about your personal saints, too—the folks who have no place on the church's calendar but who nonetheless have inspired you by their goodness.

Mark Feast Days

In Catholic tradition, children of countless generations have been given the name of a saint at baptism. That custom is not observed as often these days. You may have children named Kelly or Morgan or Sydney. It's hard to trace a heavenly connection. (Sometimes it's hard even to identify a baby's sex from its name!) If your child has a patron saint, celebrate his or her name day on that person's feast with a pizza, ice cream and cake or a special outing.

But don't limit the saints to the canonized. My friends' youngest daughter is Lori. Acknowledging the vastness of the heavenly throng, the priest who baptized her included "all the saints Lori" in the Eucharistic Prayer. Her name day is November 1, the Feast of All Saints.

A grandchild who is named for someone who hasn't been canonized needs to know what goodness inspired the choice. If the person is no longer among the living, follow the church's custom of celebrating saints' feasts on the date of their death. Borrow a living person's own birthday.

Help your child find a saint to identify as a patron, a special friend. My own patron saint is Charles Borromeo, an Italian bishop who was prominent in the movement to reform the church after the Protestant Reformation. The son of a noble Milanese family, he gave most of his means to the poor and lived in simple poverty. During a famine, he borrowed enough money to feed thousands of people every day; it took him years to repay the debt. When the plague struck Milan and most notables fled the city, he remained to care for his stricken flock.

As a child, I knew nothing of his history except his clerical status. The pious stories of the saints popular then told me only that his tongue did not decay with the rest of his body because he never told a lie. What a difficult person for a youngster with an overactive imagination to identify with!

Give your grandchild a patron who understands his or her failings. Let the poor student know that his teachers called Thomas Aquinas a "dumb ox." Joan of Arc was dismissed as a daydreamer. Introduce the kid with a hot temper to Saint Jerome, whose prickly disposition alienated everyone, but who translated the whole Bible into words the people of his time could understand. Thérèse of Lisieux refused to let even a pope tell her she was too little when she set her heart on entering the Carmelites.

Or build on the youngster's interests, talents or personality. Sports enthusiasts, for example, ought to get acquainted with Saint Paul, whose writings are full of sports metaphors (see, for example, 1 Corinthians 9:24; Philippians 3:14; 2 Timothy 4:7). Hildegarde of Bingen was a talented musician whose music has become popular in recent years. Saint Philip of Neri always had a joke to tell.

Defending an Imperfect Institution

The history of the church is not altogether pretty. Teens especially are quick to cite its failures: the Inquisition, the position of women, the greed and corruption that so offended Martin Luther, the trial of Galileo, a long history of persecuting Jews. However much we might prefer to ignore such things, they remain as stumbling blocks for our grandchildren.

Not with our ancestors did the LORD make this covenant, but with us, who are all of us here alive today. (Deuteronomy 5:3)

No enterprise run by human beings lacks flaws. Citizens of the United States rightly take pride in a long tradition of individual freedom. Yet such freedom was denied to slaves from the beginning; people of color still meet barriers in our own day. The colonies spread across a continent to build a mighty civilization, yet left what Native Americans survived in a dire state. Today we use a massive share of the world's resources while most of the earth's population goes to bed hungry.

Does all that mean we are ashamed to call ourselves Americans? Hardly!

The same is true of the church. We may rue the sins of past and present, but the church is much more than some mistaken people using power badly. Its people invented hospitals and built schools; they have fed the hungry since Saint Paul first took up a collection for the needy of Jerusalem (see 2 Corinthians 8)—an effort that continues today in the work of Catholic Relief Services and the Campaign for Human Development.

Medieval convents gave women an opportunity to live independent lives and gave them a dignity their married sisters never knew. The work of an obscure Austrian monk named Gregor Mendel gave birth to the science of genetics; a Jesuit priest-paleontologist, Teilhard de Chardin, not only advanced the theory of evolution but also gave it theological significance.

The list could go on and on. But the real beauty of the church lies closer to hand in the friends and neighbors who gather with us on Sunday. In a million quiet ways they work to make the world a gentler place.

In the long run, the church is a gathering of people who are both saints and sinners. That includes you and me—and the grandchildren we hold so dear.

For Reflection and Discussion

- *What role did the search for religious freedom play in your ancestors' story?*

- *What do you know of your forebears' personal religious journeys?*

- *What are the important milestones in your own faith-journey?*

- *Who are your favorite canonized saints?*

- *Among the people you have known, whose goodness has made a lasting personal impression on you?*

- *What do you love best about the church?*

The role of family historian need not be limited to large projects or complicated traditions. It may also mean passing down a particular recipe to your grandchildren or an especially beloved melody of a lullaby. It may also involve passing down a special holiday tradition or making copies of a special photograph.... As a family historian, you are your children's and grandchildren's bridge to the past and they are your link with immortality. (Dr. Ruth Westheimer and Steven Kaplan, *Grandparenthood,* Routledge, 2000)

"For inquire now of bygone generations,
and consider what their ancestors
have found....
Will they not teach you and tell you
and utter words out of their understanding?" (Job 8:8,10)

Conclusion

We began by looking at the limits we face as grandparents. Those limits are imposed by the fact that the young people who have such a hold on our hearts have not been entrusted to our care, but to their parents'.

But neither is that the whole story. Our grandchildren ultimately belong to our children no more than our children belong to us. The newest generation will, like all before them, eventually up and go their own way. But, like all their elders, they will remain in God's hands.

We help them along their way with our love, our example, our stories and, most of all, with our prayers. And we rest secure in an ancient promise handed down to us by our ancestors in faith:

> For the LORD is good;
>   his steadfast love endures forever,
>   and his faithfulness to all generations.
>   (Psalm 100:5)